PITTSBURGH STEELERS

BY TOM GLAVE

The Child's World

Published by The Child's World®
1980 Lookout Drive • Mankato, MN 56003-1705
800-599-READ • www.childsworld.com

Acknowledgments
The Child's World®: Mary Berendes, Publishing Director
Red Line Editorial: Editorial direction
The Design Lab: Design
Amnet: Production

Design Element: Dean Bertoncelj/Shutterstock Images
Photographs ©: Gene Puskar/AP Images, cover; AP Images,
5, 19; Winslow Townson/AP Images, 7; Harry Cabluck/
AP Images, 9, 17; Nick Wass/AP Images, 11; Sean Pavone/
Shutterstock Images, 13; Gene J. Puskar/AP Images, 14–15;
Rusty Kennedy/AP Images, 21; Kevin Terrell/AP Images, 23;
ZumaPress/Icon Sportswire, 25; Ric Tapia/Icon Sportswire,
27; Robert Seale/TSN/ZumaPress/Icon Sportswire, 29

ISBN 9781631439940
LCCN 2014959699

Printed in the United States of America
Mankato, MN
February, 2016
PA02311

ABOUT THE AUTHOR

Tom Glave grew up watching football on TV and playing it in the field next to his house. He learned to write about sports at the University of Missouri–Columbia and has written for newspapers in New Jersey, Missouri, Arkansas, and Texas. He lives near Houston, Texas, and cannot wait to play backyard football with his kids Tommy, Lucas, and Allison.

TABLE OF CONTENTS

GO, STEELERS!

The Pittsburgh Steelers have six **Super Bowl** trophies. That is more than any other team. The Steelers set that record after the 2008 season. Pittsburgh has won back-to-back Super Bowls twice. No other team has done that. The Steelers dominated the 1970s. They won four Super Bowls that decade. Fans in "The Steel City" love their team. Let's meet the Steelers.

Pittsburgh's "Steel Curtain" is known as one of the toughest defenses in NFL history.

4

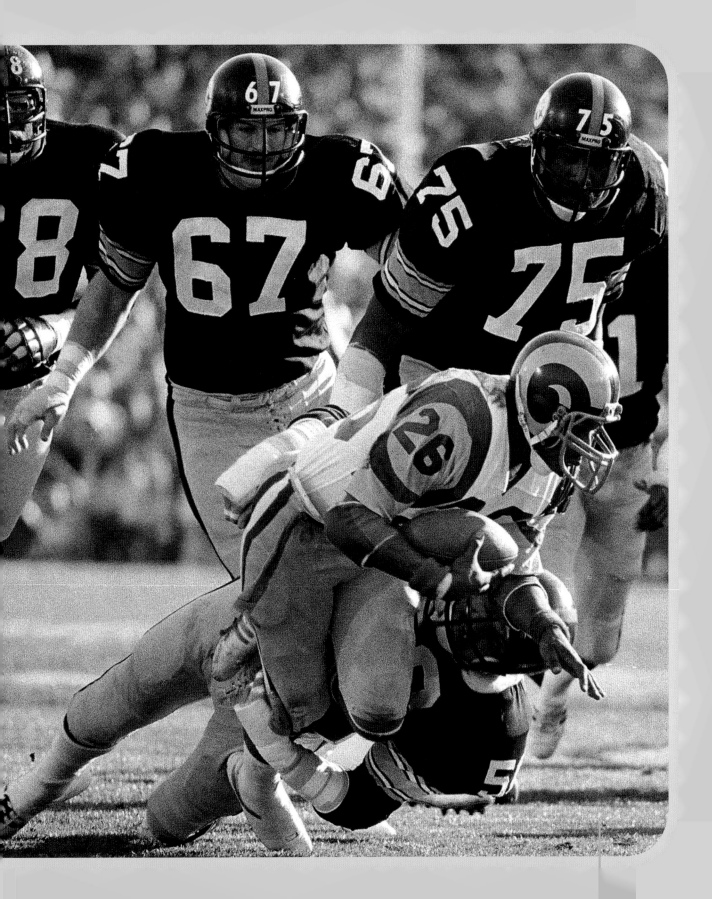

WHO ARE THE STEELERS?

The Pittsburgh Steelers play in the National Football **League** (NFL). They are one of the 32 teams in the NFL. The NFL includes the American Football Conference (AFC) and the National Football Conference (NFC). The winner of the AFC plays the winner of the NFC in the Super Bowl. The Steelers play in the North Division of the AFC. They have played in eight Super Bowls. No team has played in more through 2014.

Quarterback Ben Roethlisberger celebrates a touchdown in Pittsburgh's 27–23 Super Bowl win over the Arizona Cardinals on February 1, 2009.

WHERE THEY CAME FROM

The Steelers were created in 1933. They were first called the Pirates. The team shared Forbes Field with Pittsburgh's baseball team. It was also called the Pirates. The football team was renamed the Steelers in 1940. Pittsburgh won seven division titles in the 1970s. It also won four Super Bowls. No other team had done that. The Steelers won the championship after the 1974, 1975, 1978, and 1979 seasons. They also won after the 2005 and 2008 seasons.

Coach Chuck Noll (right) led the Steelers to four Super Bowl titles in the 1970s.

WHO THEY PLAY

The Pittsburgh Steelers play 16 games each season. With so few games, each one is important. Every year, the Steelers play two games against each of the other three teams in their division. Those teams are the Baltimore Ravens, Cincinnati Bengals, and Cleveland Browns. The Steelers also play six other teams from the AFC and four from the NFC. The Ravens and Steelers are **rivals**. They have tough AFC North battles. Sometimes they even meet in the **playoffs**. The Steelers and Oakland Raiders played intense games during the 1970s.

Some say the rivalry between the Steelers and the Ravens is the best in the NFL.

WHERE THEY PLAY

The Steelers first played in Forbes Field. The Steelers also played some games at Pitt Stadium. That is the University of Pittsburgh's football field. The Steelers and Pirates left Forbes Field in 1970. They both moved to Three Rivers Stadium. Now the Steelers play at Heinz Field. It opened in 2001. It holds 65,500 fans. Heinz is a food company. It is known for its ketchup. Heinz Field's scoreboard has two giant bottles. They pretend to pour ketchup when Pittsburgh enters the **red zone**. The stadium includes the Great Hall. It has copies of the team's Super Bowl trophies. It also has other pieces of Steelers history.

Heinz Field has been the scene for many memorable moments since the Steelers started playing there in 2001.

THE FOOTBALL FIELD

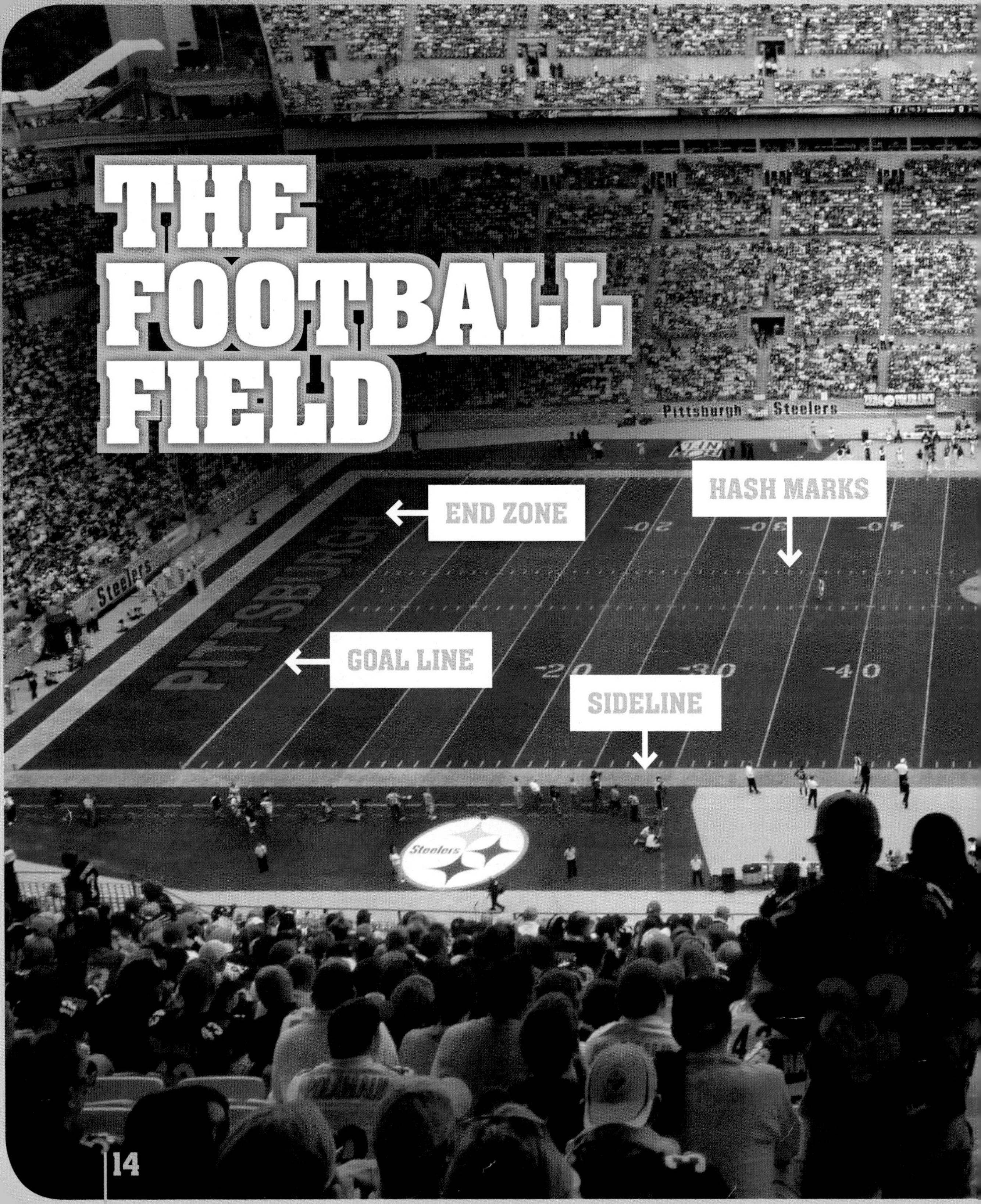

END ZONE

HASH MARKS

GOAL LINE

SIDELINE

GOAL POST →

MIDFIELD ←

20-YARD LINE

BENCH AREA

END LINE →

Pittsburgh Steelers

BIG DAYS

The Steelers have had some great moments in their history. Here are three of the greatest:

1972—The Steelers were in the playoffs. They played the Oakland Raiders on December 23. Oakland led 7-6 with 22 seconds left. Pittsburgh was on its own 40-yard line. Running back Franco Harris caught a deflected pass. He then ran and scored a touchdown. Pittsburgh won 13-7 on "The Immaculate Reception." It was the first postseason win in **franchise** history.

1979—The Steelers won the AFC Central. It was their seventh division title in eight years. Then they beat the Los Angeles Rams in the Super Bowl. It was Pittsburgh's fourth Super Bowl win in six years.

Running back Franco Harris runs for the end zone after making "The Immaculate Reception" in Pittsburgh's 13-7 win over the Oakland Raiders on December 23, 1972.

2006—The 2005 Steelers barely made the playoffs. But then they made the Super Bowl. They met the Seattle Seahawks on February 5. Steelers running back Willie Parker scored on a 75-yard run. Wide receiver Antwaan Randle El threw a touchdown pass. Pittsburgh won 21-10.

TOUGH DAYS

Football is a hard game. Even the best teams have rough games and seasons. Here are some of the toughest times in Steelers history:

1955—The Steelers drafted quarterback Johnny Unitas. But they did not think he was ready to lead. So Pittsburgh released him before the season. Unitas went to the Baltimore Colts. He became one of the best quarterbacks ever. He won three NFL Most Valuable Player (MVP) awards.

1969—The Steelers won their first game. But then they lost their final 13. Pittsburgh allowed almost 29 points per game. That was worst in the NFL. The 1-13 record is the worst in team history.

The 1969 Steelers team that only won one game scored ten points or less six times.

1998—Pittsburgh played the Detroit Lions on Thanksgiving. The game was tied after four quarters. Before **overtime**, there is a coin flip. The winner decides who starts with the ball. Pittsburgh running back Jerome Bettis called it correctly. But referee Phil Luckett misheard the call. The Lions got the ball first. They scored to win the game.

MEET THE FANS

Steelers fans wave gold towels during games. They are called "Terrible Towels." The towels were created by radio announcer Myron Cope during the 1975 playoffs. The Steelers won the Super Bowl after that season. Pittsburgh has sold out every home game since the 1972 season. The city is known for its steel companies. So the Steelers' mascot is named Steely McBeam. He wears a hardhat and carries a steel beam.

Pittsburgh fans love waving their "Terrible Towels" during big moments in Steelers games.

HEROES THEN

Quarterback Terry Bradshaw was Super Bowl MVP twice. He led the Steelers to all four of their 1970s titles. Franco Harris was a powerful running back. He was the MVP of the team's first Super Bowl. Defensive tackle Joe Greene was known as "Mean Joe Greene." He was the leader of Pittsburgh's 1970s defense. It was called "The Steel Curtain." All three of those players are in the Pro Football Hall of Fame. Wide receiver Hines Ward spent his entire career with Pittsburgh. He was a great blocker and pass catcher. Jerome Bettis was a big running back. He was nicknamed "The Bus." Bettis played with Pittsburgh from 1996 to 2005. He made the **Pro Bowl** four times.

The Steelers made the playoffs in 10 of quarterback Terry Bradshaw's 14 NFL seasons.

HEROES NOW

Quarterback Ben Roethlisberger was a rookie in 2004. He won his first 14 starts in the NFL. He has led the Steelers to two Super Bowl wins. Le'Veon Bell was another great rookie. He joined the Steelers in 2013. That year, he broke Franco Harris's team rookie record with 1,259 yards from scrimmage. Receiver Antonio Brown set a record in 2011. He became the first NFL player to have 1,000 receiving yards and 1,000 return yards in the same season. Linebacker Lawrence Timmons dominates the middle of the field on defense. He made his first Pro Bowl in 2014.

Running back Le'Veon Bell made his first Pro Bowl in 2014.

GEARING UP

NFL players wear team uniforms. They wear helmets and pads to keep them safe. Cleats help them make quick moves and run fast. Some players wear extra gear for protection.

THE FOOTBALL

NFL footballs are made of leather. Under the leather is a lining that fills with air to give the ball its shape. The leather has bumps or "pebbles." These help players grip the ball. Laces help players control their throws. Footballs are also called "pigskins" because some of the first balls were made from pig bladders. Today they are made of leather from cows.

Antonio Brown is a threat to score as a receiver or a kick returner.

HELMET

CHIN STRAP

SHOULDER PADS

GLOVES

CLEATS

FOOTBALL

SPORTS STATS

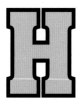

Here are some of the all-time career records for the Pittsburgh Steelers. All the stats are through the 2014 season.

PASSING YARDS

Ben Roethlisberger 39,057

Terry Bradshaw 27,989

RUSHING YARDS

Franco Harris 11,950

Jerome Bettis 10,571

INTERCEPTIONS

Mel Blount 57

Jack Butler 52

TOTAL TOUCHDOWNS

Franco Harris 100

Hines Ward 86

SACKS

Jason Gildon 77

James Harrison 69.5

POINTS

Gary Anderson 1,343

Jeff Reed 919

Wide receiver Hines Ward was the MVP of Pittsburgh's Super Bowl win after the 2005 season.

RECEPTIONS

Hines Ward 1,000

John Stallworth 537

GLOSSARY

franchise a team that is part of a professional sports league

league an organization of sports teams that compete against each other

overtime extra time that is played when teams are tied at the end of four quarters

playoffs a series of games after the regular season that decides which two teams play in the Super Bowl

Pro Bowl the NFL's All-Star game, in which the best players in the league compete

red zone the area on the field between the 20-yard line and the goal line

rivals teams whose games bring out the greatest emotion between the players and the fans on both sides

Super Bowl the championship game of the NFL, played between the winners of the AFC and the NFC

FIND OUT MORE

IN THE LIBRARY

Editors of Sports Illustrated. *Sports Illustrated Pittsburgh Steelers: Pride in Black and Gold.* New York: Time Home Entertainment, 2012.

Frisch, Aaron. *Super Bowl Champions: Pittsburgh Steelers.* Mankato, MN: Creative Education, 2014.

Grdnic, Dale. *Tales from the Pittsburgh Steelers Sideline.* New York: Sports Publishing, 2013.

ON THE WEB

Visit our Web site for links about the Pittsburgh Steelers:

childsworld.com/links

Note to Parents, Teachers, and Librarians: We routinely verify our Web links to make sure they are safe and active sites. So encourage your readers to check them out!

INDEX